The  Awakening Of Humanity

What You Need to Know

By

Michael Moriarty

©2017 by Michael Moriarty

All rights reserved.

ISBN 978-1-387-19629-6

Email: moriartym248@gmail.com

Contents

1. You Created This Mess (Surprise!): The Law of Attraction—Page 5

2. The Way Out of the Mess: Conscious Creation of Your Life—Page 11

3. Disclosure, Allowing, and Your Sovereignty—Page 17

4. Open Contact: YOU Must Change—Page 21

5. The Higher Purpose of the Darkness—Page 25

6. Karma, Forgiveness, and the Law of Attraction—Page 29

7. Rise of the Divine Feminine: Restoration of Balance—Page 33

8. Maldek and the Inner Earth—Page 37

9. The Repopulation of Earth—Page 41

10. The New Earth—Page 47

Chapter One

You Created This Mess (Surprise!): The Law of Attraction

In this chapter, I have two goals. First, to show how each individual Human Being is the creator of his/her reality. Second, to show how, if one person did not realize this but another did, the second person could use that disparity in knowledge to—*seemingly*—manipulate the first person to create realities that seem to serve the second person (while seemingly harming the first).

Let's keep this as simple as possible. For our purposes, we will define one Universal Law: the Law of Attraction. The Law of Attraction (LOA), simply stated, says that *that which is like unto itself, is drawn.* The essence of how the LOA applies to you is the recognition that this Universal Law acts on vibration and that all things vibrate. More to the point: your thoughts vibrate. Things— other thoughts, objects, events, circumstances, people-- with a similar vibration to your thought will be attracted to you, by you, through your thought. The LOA is acting— always acting, for there is never a time when the Law is not operative—on your current thought. It doesn't matter if your thought is about what happened in the past; about what you are observing in the present; or about something you are imagining regarding your future. The LOA is acting on the thought you are having in this "now" moment, in each "now" moment.

You get the (vibrational) essence of what you think about or focus your attention upon, whether you want it or not. What you predominantly think about will cause your predominant vibrational "set point" (or your *point of attraction*). Since a belief is just a thought that you think a lot, another way of stating this is: you create/attract your reality through your beliefs.

Notice that this implies that it is *not* that "seeing is believing"; in truth, it is that "believing is seeing". A further implication of this line of thought is that no reality/experience is any more real, basic, or fundamental than any other. Each thought or belief creates/attracts "evidence" or "facts" that seem to justify the correctness of the belief but, if the belief were to be changed, the so-called evidence or facts would also change (and seem to justify the new belief). In short, there is no reality outside of yourself: any experience that you have has been created/attracted by you through your beliefs. Life is not something that just happens to you; nor does it come to you from outside yourself. Physical reality is a mirror that shows you what you most-strongly believe (tells you what your point of attraction is).

I ask you, "Can anyone else think for you"? No, they cannot. Thus, they cannot vibrate for you. Hence, they cannot attract or create your life experiences for you. You are not only the creator/attractor of your own life experience (through what you think about or focus your attention upon), but you are the *sole* creator/ attractor of that experience. We might say that all your realities or experiences are invited to you, by you, through your thoughts or beliefs.

All realities or experiences are by invitation only—the invitation of the experiencer. For two or more people to interact, at all, then, requires each person involved in the experience to agree to the interaction. The "agreement" or "invitation" comes in the form of having similar beliefs (which the LOA will act upon, bringing the parties together in a co-creation). If so, then how could anyone be a victim? They cannot be: each person is free to think or believe as he/she chooses and, hence, to create/attract as he/she chooses. Also: how could anyone save another? They cannot: they cannot create/attract for the other, as they cannot think for them. We will come back to these important conclusions.

Now, let's imagine a scenario in which there are two people, person A and person B. Further, imagine that B realizes that each of these two persons, A and B, creates/attracts his/her own reality; but, person A does not realize this. If person B were so inclined, he could use this disparity in knowledge to his seeming advantage: if he could persuade A to believe that A should serve B in whatever ways that B desires, then the reality created/attracted (through the LOA) by that shared belief will reflect that belief: A will serve B.

Taking this imagined scenario one step further, let's say that A serves B but, over time, comes to realize that he does not enjoy doing so. What is to stop A from ceasing to serve B? Nothing. In this situation, how can B keep his servant A? Once again, B could use the disparity in knowledge between himself and A regarding the truth that A, like B, creates/attracts his own reality through his beliefs, to—seemingly—keep A in servitude. If B could persuade A to believe, for example, that he, A, is helpless to change his reality, that reality is something that comes to one from outside oneself and that one has little control over it, then the reality created/attracted by *that* belief will faithfully reflect that belief: A will serve B.

Notice that, as long as A continues to subscribe to the belief that he cannot substantially alter his reality, his reality will not substantially alter: he will continue to serve B. To be sure, he may resent his servitude to B, but he will serve B. Notice, too, the double-bind that A is in. On the one hand, if he thinks that he should serve B, his reality will reflect that belief: he will serve B. On the other hand, if he focuses his attention upon his *not wanting to serve B*, his reality will reflect that thought: he will attract more opportunities to *not want to serve B* (i.e., he will continue to serve B). Remember: anything you think about/focus your attention upon you are attracting to yourself—whether you want it or not. With the set of beliefs that A now holds, he is—seemingly—locked-into serving B forever. In such a circumstance, with the beliefs that he holds, A may very well see himself as a victim, and B as his victimizer. B, however, knows that he is not a victimizer and that A is not his victim.

Does this sound familiar? In our example, we limited ourselves to just two persons; however, we need not have. Imagine extending this example to include thousands, millions, or even billions of people on Earth serving B (or a small group of people like B). Does that sound familiar to you? This is the situation that billions of Human Beings on Earth today find themselves in.

But, let's go back to the beginning of our example with A and B. How did B persuade A to serve him? The answer is that he didn't. A *chose* to serve B. We'll come back to the intriguing question of why A would make such a choice. First, however, let us answer the question of why A continues, over time, to serve B. Perhaps it was so long ago that the choice to serve B was made *consciously* by A (or his ancestors) that A does not realize that he has a choice. In addition, since A does not understand how he is getting what he is getting, in terms of his life experiences, then he does not understand how to (seemingly) free himself. Finally, since A believes that life is something outside himself that he has little control over, he, in all likelihood, will resign himself to his "fate". Anything else would seem pointless to him.

Why did A, originally, choose to serve B? If he hadn't, then he and B would not have had any shared beliefs and, so, they would not have been able to co-create a reality together: each would not have been in the experience of the other *at all*. What could A possibly gain from an arrangement where he, seemingly, is enslaved to B? Consider this carefully: the reality of (seeming) enslavement that A co-creates with B reflects back to A his most-strongly held belief. What belief? That he is unworthy to rule himself, that he cannot trust himself to make the correct choices in his life. This belief is very close to the heart of A; it must be, for it is what leads A to create/attract a reality of (seeming) servitude and suffering for himself. Where did he ever get the idea that he is unworthy of his sovereignty, of his creator hood? Perhaps, in an earlier time, before B came along, *A made some poor choices that led to absolutely horrific results and the pain and guilt of what he had done is seared onto his psyche.* He is responsible for the Fall of Atlantis, with the consequent destruction of much of the life on the surface of the Earth (and nearly destroyed Gaia, herself). This event occurred so far back in time that he no longer consciously remembers it, yet his psyche carries the knowledge, still.

Note, too, that the deeper that A goes into (seeming) servitude to B, the greater will be the sense of (seeming) liberation when it comes. This "game of limitation" played by A and B serves A in that way, as well. It is clear what B gets out of this game: he gets to experience (seeming) mastery/dominion over another. But, never forget that B *is* serving A, and that B *knows* that he is not a victimizer and that A is not a victim. And B is correct.

The stakes of this "game of limitation" have, at this point, become very high: if this "game" goes on much longer, there is a danger of something similar to what happened with the Fall of Atlantis being repeated (by the misuse of HAARP technology). In addition, the "game" is very clearly harming the ecosystems of the Earth (and of those civilizations which reside within the Earth, although this is less well-known to surface dwellers), and threatens to harm other planets and star systems, as the "game" is now, with the advancement of technology, spreading throughout the Solar System and beyond.

No one—and no technology--can save or rescue A from his (seeming) predicament. To play this "game of limitation" with B, A must deny that he is the sole creator/attractor of his reality. Nonetheless, he still is. His failure to accept responsibility—100% responsibility—for the creation of his life experiences is the fundamental issue. And the price of his denial of his creator hood powers is becoming unsustainable.

Strange "game"…the only way to win is not to play.

You are A. *You are the one who created this mess on Earth. You are responsible for creating it; you are responsible for cleaning it up. Only you can.*

Chapter Two

The Way Out of the Mess: Conscious Creation of Your Life

In this chapter, I will introduce the concept of your Higher Self, and will show that, by paying attention to how you feel, and by always reaching for the best-feeling thought that you have access to in the moment, you can be, do, or have anything you wish to be, do, or have.

We have seen that the fundamental premise of reality-creation/attraction is that *you get what you think about/focus your attention upon, whether you want it or not.* That being the case, it would be wise to be aware of what you are thinking about or focusing your attention upon, from moment-to-moment. "Does this mean that I have to constantly monitor my thoughts?" you ask. Since the LOA is acting upon your thoughts, bringing you similar thoughts, monitoring your thoughts could become a challenging task. But, in any case, it's not necessary. Instead, simply pay attention to the way you feel.

In addition to the you-that-you-know, this physical you that you think of when you think of yourself, there is another part of you—by far, the greatest part of your energy—that remains focused in the non-physical realm. The non-physical part of you is known by many names (your God Self; your Inner Being; to name but a few). However, we will choose to call it your Higher Self. The name is not important; what is important is to know that your Higher Self communicates with the physical you.

The communication comes in many forms; but, for our purposes, we wish to note that your emotions—your feelings—are, in all cases, communication from your Higher Self. This *emotional guidance from your Higher*

Self lets you know, in each moment, whether you are creating or mis-creating. That is, if you think, say, or do anything that is *not* in vibrational harmony with your overall intent, you will feel negative emotion. That bad feeling is communication from your Higher Self letting you know that, if you continue to focus your attention upon or think about what you are currently focusing upon/thinking about, the LOA will manifest it into your experience (*as* your experience)—and you will *not* be happy with the experience. Similarly, if you think, say, or do anything that *is* in vibrational harmony with your overall intent, you will feel positive emotion. That good feeling is communication from your Higher Self telling you that, if you continue to focus upon/think about the subject in question, the LOA will manifest it into your life—and you *will* be happy with the experience.

Thus, a monitoring of your thoughts is not necessary for you to create the life you wish to live. Instead, by paying attention to how you feel you will know the direction of your creating. Furthermore, although each and every thought has creative potential, the thoughts that evoke powerful emotion—regardless of whether it is positive emotion or negative emotion—will manifest more quickly than the thoughts that evoke little emotion. Thus, if you want something—a person, an object, money, circumstances, whatever—to manifest quickly, focus your attention upon/think about that subject more frequently. As the LOA responds to what you are thinking about by bringing to you similar thoughts, the thought will become more powerful and will evoke more powerful emotion.

Imagination is one of your greatest gifts for, if you wish to experience something other than What-Is, *you must allow yourself to imagine something other* than What-Is. If you continue to observe or think about What-Is, you will only continue to create/attract more circumstances that are similar to your current circumstances (What-Is).

Related to this is the understanding that circumstances don't matter; only your state of Being (your dominant vibrational offering, or point of attraction) matters. Your circumstances don't create/attract your circumstances; neither do they determine your state of Being (you are free to choose what to think about/focus your attention upon, which is what determines your point of attraction). Your state of Being is what creates/attracts your circumstances. As you begin to shift your point of attraction by thinking about/focusing on only what you desire to experience, there may be a period in which your previous vibrational offering still dominates within you. Hence, during that period you will continue to create/attract more of What-Is. However, if you continue to think about/focus upon only what you desire, your point of attraction and, thus, your circumstances—the "facts", the "evidence of your senses", What-Is—will change to reflect your desires.

Your Higher Self is responsible for translating your point of attraction into the experiences that you have; it is the mechanism that, in accordance with the LOA, actually carries out that task. Thus, you do not need to concern yourself with *how* what you want will come about. Your Higher Self will take care of the details for you. Your work is only to decide what you would like to experience and to think about/ focus upon that. You are not here to create the life that you desire through your *actions*. Instead, your actions are meant to be a way in which you *enjoy* that which you have created through *thought*.

It is important to notice that every subject that you think about/focus upon is, really, two subjects: what you want and what you don't want (or the *absence* of what you want). So, if you think about/focus upon the absence of what you want, you will create/attract the absence of what you want (i.e., you won't get what you want). But, once again, your emotional guidance from your Higher Self will help you to sort things out. Just pay attention to how you feel and, if you feel good, then you know that you are thinking about/focusing upon what you want; if you feel bad, then you know that you are thinking about/focusing upon what you do *not* want (or the *absence* of what you want).

Notice, too, this important conclusion: since you activate the vibration within yourself of anything that you focus upon or think about; and since the LOA will bring to you the vibrational essence of what you focus upon or think about; the way to *not* get what you do *not* want is to focus your attention upon/think about what you *do* want. *You attract to you anything that you oppose.*

It is true that the experiences that you are having today were created/attracted to you, by you, through the thoughts that you have had before today. Very little of what you are living today is a result only of the thoughts that you are having today. It's also true that, because the LOA is making more powerful any thought that you continue to think about, there is a momentum to your thoughts. So, if you have been thinking about/focusing upon something that you don't want for some time, you will have a relatively large negative momentum behind that subject. However, it is not necessary to attempt to reverse that momentum. Instead, just begin thinking about/focusing your attention upon what you *do* want. In time, the balance of your vibrational offering will shift in the direction of what you desire. As a consequence, your reality will more and more reflect that shift in your vibrational set-point (your point of attraction) by bringing to you more and more of what you do want, and less and less of what you don't want. Eventually, what you don't want will no longer be a part of your reality.

As you know, if you find yourself feeling very badly, it is very difficult to immediately think thoughts that feel a lot better. What you may not realize is that this is because the LOA can, and will, bring you thoughts that are similar to your current thought, but cannot bring you a thought that is very different from your current thought (remember: like, vibrationally, attracts like). So, if you find yourself in such a situation, what should you do to change your point of attraction so that you may begin attracting what you do want and not what you don't? Simple: reach for the best-feeling thought that you *do* have access to in the moment. Thinking *that* thought for a while will shift, albeit slightly, your point of attraction in the direction that you desire. Then, think a thought that feels slightly better still. If you continue in this manner, you will eventually move your point of attraction all the way to where you want it to be (so that you may create/attract exactly what you wish to experience).

Reflecting further upon the idea that a thought that you think or focus upon will gain momentum as you continue to think about or focus upon it, you can understand that you are, with the thoughts that you think today, creating/attracting experiences that you will live tomorrow (or one week from now; or one year; etc.). It is much easier, by paying attention to how you feel and always reaching for the best-feeling thought that you have access to in the moment, to avoid creating/attracting experiences that you don't want than it is to deal with such unwanted experiences *after* they have already manifested. However, if you do manifest an experience that you do not desire, deal with it however you choose, but do not leave your thoughts where they are or you will continue to create/attract more unpleasant experiences. Start thinking about/focusing upon what you *do* want.

If your objective is to always feel good, you will achieve everything that you desire. In always reaching for the best-feeling thought that you have access to in the moment, you will find the thoughts that will create/attract everything that you desire. And, in all of that, you will feel good. Thus, *there is nothing more important than that you feel good—now.*

O.K., now you know exactly what to do to clean up the mess that you created on this planet. If you do this, the "game of limitation" will be over. In addition, you will experience (your version of) "Paradise on Earth".

"But, wait!" you say. "It can't be as simple as that. What about B? How do I get him to change his ways?"

The answer is that you don't, and that you can't. But, then, you don't need to.

Chapter Three

Disclosure, Allowing, and Your Sovereignty

In this chapter, I illustrate—using Disclosure as an example—that the choices that others make can in no way harm you. Further, by believing that you must depend upon others to bring to you the life that you desire to live, you give away your sovereignty—your creator hood powers—to those others. This belief stymies your evolution. Finally, I show that you can only experience total freedom by being an allower of others.

To illustrate, let's use the Disclosure of the Extraterrestrial Presence (and associated technologies and programs) on planet Earth as an example. In this case, then, B represents the Cabal/Illuminati (or the World Management Team, or whatever you wish to call them). If the Cabal/Illuminati wishes to continue to play the "game of limitation", including withholding Disclosure, nothing that you can say or do is likely to make them choose otherwise. But, *you don't need the Cabal/Illuminati's permission* to create for yourself/attract to yourself Disclosure experiences. Remember: you are the *sole* creator/attractor of your reality. *All* of it, *all* the time. You have never needed their permission for anything that you have experienced. You have invited all of your experiences to you by what you have predominately thought about/focused your attention upon. Another way of saying this is that you have created/attracted all of your experiences through your beliefs.

Do you see the irony in the situation? By believing that you are the helpless victims of the Cabal/Illuminati, you have created—through that belief—the experience of being helpless victims of the Cabal/Illuminati. Their apparent power over you is just that—apparent. If you chose to believe the opposite--that you are the sole creators/attractors of your own life experiences--then *that* is what your experiences would reflect. But, in that case, who would you blame for your problems? (Do you see how the Cabal/Illuminati is serving you in this way—*as an excuse*?)

Further, by believing that you must have the Cabal/Illuminati's permission to experience Disclosure (or anything else), you lock yourself into a situation where you may not evolve further. Indeed, in such a circumstance, the Cabal/Illuminati may *never* choose to stop playing the "game of limitation". To evolve further, then--at some point--you must jettison that belief. Why not do so now? Can you, the Earth, the Solar System, the Galaxy, and beyond, afford for you *not* to do so now?

There are no shortcuts up the Spiral of Light. Let these words serve as a warning to you. You cannot indefinitely assign responsibility for your evolution to others while, at the same time, expecting to evolve. *You must do the work* required for your evolution, or you will not evolve. What does it mean to "do the work"? It means, primarily, accepting responsibility for your creator hood powers, for the truth that each individual is the sole creator/attractor of his/her life experience. Remember: physical reality exists as a mirror to show you what you most-strongly believe. Thus, physical reality is a kind of living feedback, meant to show you, at any moment, *what you are.* This is how you can judge whether or not you are moving up the Spiral of Light back to the One Infinite Creator. Do you see reflected in the mirror of your physical reality the Unconditional Love and Wisdom of the Creator?

When you accept that everything reflected in the mirror has been put there by you, then—and only then—will you be motivated to make any desired changes in yourself. If you deny that the reflection is your own, how would you know what changes to make in yourself? And why would you bother?

If you do not understand how it is that you are getting what you are getting, in terms of your life experiences, then, of course, you would be concerned about what others are intending, thinking, feeling, saying, and doing. But, when you understand that you are the inviter, through what you think about/focus your attention upon, of each and every one of those life experiences, then you know that nothing that anyone intends, thinks, feels, says, or does can assert itself into your life experience without your invitation. No one, and no thing, can threaten you or your happiness. If you don't want to experience something, simply choose to not give your thought, or the focus of your attention, to it.

You are not here on Earth to get others to intend, think, feel, say, or do as you do. No. You are here to decide what you would like to experience; to think about/focus your attention upon *that;* and, thereby, create/attract that. At the same time, you recognize that others are creating/attracting their own life experiences through *their* choices as to what to think about/ focus *their* attention upon. Knowing that they, like you, are the sole creators/attractors of their life experiences; and that their choices don't threaten you in any way; you realize that it is not necessary for you, in order to protect yourself, to concern yourself with their choices and that you do not have the power to create/attract their life experiences for them, anyway (only *they* can do that). You must allow them their choices, whether you want to or not.

Let us make an important point of clarification. There is a profound difference between *tolerating* and *allowing.* When you are tolerating someone or something, you are experiencing negative emotion and, hence, you are mis-creating. That is, when you are tolerating, you are creating/attracting more of that which you do *not* want. On the other hand, when you are allowing someone or something, you are not feeling negative emotion and, hence, you are not creating/attracting that which you do not want.

Only when you are an allower do you experience *total freedom*—freedom from any experience that you don't want and freedom from any negative response to any experience that you do not approve of. Thus, allowing is the greatest state of Being that one can achieve on a consistent, long-term basis.

Chapter Four

Open Contact: YOU Must Change

In this chapter, I will explain why it is that, for Open Contact with benevolent extraterrestrials and non-physical Beings to occur, several conditions must be established. These conditions require that all Human Beings presently on Earth "do the work" demanded for their own, individual Spiritual evolution (and most, currently, are not doing so). Furthermore, I show that it is an error to think that Open Contact is about the acquisition, by the public, of advanced technology. Rather, it is about becoming more loving.

Wherever you go, you take yourself with you. If the mass of Humanity treats their own planet, Earth, as badly as they undeniably do, then why would anyone believe that they would treat any other planet in the Universe any better? If the mass of Humanity treat their own brothers and sisters—their fellow Humans—as badly as they undeniably do, then why would anyone believe that they would treat any other race of Beings in the Universe any better? The collective of Human Beings on Earth would wreak havoc on the Solar System and the wider Galaxy, were Humans—at their present level of consciousness--allowed to travel, in large numbers, throughout the Solar System and Galaxy.

Thus, it is not just the Cabal/Illuminati that keeps space travel technology out of the hands of the average Human. Benevolent extraterrestrials and non-physical Beings are doing so, too—albeit for different reasons than the Cabal/Illuminati.

From the above, it is evident that, for Open Contact to occur, the bulk of Human Beings on Earth must become *more loving—more loving toward the Earth (and the plants and animals that they share the Earth with); toward their Inner Earth brothers and sisters; and toward each other.* They must become the *kinds of Beings* who would *never* abuse or misuse great power, were they to acquire it (does anyone remember Atlantis and its Fall?). Yes, the advanced technology will, eventually, come to the mass of Humanity. First, however, Humanity must *prove itself capable of handling that kind of power responsibly.* The clamor, by so many, for the release of advanced technology without due consideration to Humanity's current level of consciousness—its lack of compassion and respect for Life—is proof-positive that those doing the clamoring have not even *begun* to accept responsibility for their creator hood powers.

In short, each Human Being must "do the work" required for his/her Spiritual growth. He/she must accept 100% responsibility for his/her own life experiences. Any Human Being who refuses to accept total responsibility for each and every aspect of his/her reality is *refusing to be honest about what kind of Being that he/she is.* This means, for example, that he/she could be the kind of Being who would abuse or misuse advanced technology, were he/she to acquire it, but still believe that he/she were not such a person. Further, it would mean that they would, likely, see no reason to become more loving and, thus, would not likely do so.

Part-and-parcel of accepting responsibility for your creations is eliminating the fears and traumas within you—creations that you are not so proud of and, indeed, are afraid to face. These are the dark emotions that you have hidden from yourself, precisely so that you wouldn't have to face them. In addition, many of you believe that it is somehow improper or inappropriate for you to experience these emotions. To evolve—or even to survive, now that the stakes of the "game of limitation" have gotten so high—

you have to bring these emotions into the Light of your conscious awareness. If you don't, these emotions will prevent you from travelling up the Spiral of Light.

What is the Darkness if not the absence (the lack) of the Light? Simply by shining the Light of your conscious awareness into the dark corners of your Being, you dissolve that darkness. You become freed to evolve up the Spiral, back to the Creator of All That Is.

Remember, during this process, to be kind to yourself, to be gentle with yourself. Be understanding of, and compassionate to, others, as well: they are travelling the same challenging road as you.

The path *without* the Earth's atmosphere starts *within* each of us. As within, so without. Benevolent ETs will not be coming to you; *you* will be going to them.

I ask you: if we are *all* children of the same One Infinite Creator, then are we not *all* brothers and sisters? *Not* some of us, but not others. *Not* those who are "good", but not those who are "evil". *All.*

Chapter Five

The Higher Purpose of the Darkness

In this chapter, I explain that the forces of Darkness are not outside of All That Is, but an integral part of the Whole. Without polarity--without the dynamic interplay of Love and Fear, Good and Evil--there is no free will choice. Lucifer, symbol of opposition to God, in truth, serves you, as an individual and Humanity, as a collective. When you understand this, you acquire gratitude for the great gifts that the dark warriors have given you. Only then will your Love grow so large that it can even encompass those that you have, heretofore, hated and feared.

How can anyone or anything be outside of All That Is? They cannot be. Thus, Darkness is the reflection of the Light of God, a *part* of God. Polarity is part of the Divine Plan and the fabric of the Universe. Without polarity—hot/cold; good/evil; love/fear; etc.—how could you choose? You could not. *Without the Dark, the Light has no meaning (and vice versa).*

Without the devil, you would not have the free-will choice that gives purpose to your life and to Life, itself. If you only knew the Light, where would you find the motivation to move up the Spiral of Light toward the Godhead? Indeed, without the challenges you face, why would you ever have individuated from the One to begin with? And, if you had not done so, that One could not create new experiences (since the One creates through individual Beings): Creation would cease. You exist, as an individual Being (as a Godspark), to participate in the expansion of All That Is—by separating from the Creator; by making choices; by facing challenges created by those choices; and, by consistently choosing the Light in the face of such challenges, to return up the Spiral of Light to the One Eternal Flame.

You, through your free-will choices have created/attracted to you all the so-called "evil" that you have experienced, through what you have been predominantly thinking about/focusing your attention upon. Reflect upon what is written above. Do you see how those who choose the darkness have served you and the Creator? Thank them. Love them. They are your brothers and sisters.

In truth, you and they have, each, agreed to co-create those experiences together, albeit for different reasons. It is like a great, Cosmic play in which you each participate. You have chosen to play the role of the "good guy", while they have chosen to play the role of the "bad guy". These are just roles that you and they adopt, temporarily (everything is temporary when seen from the perspective of the no-time of Eternity). Tell the truth, now: doesn't the bad guy have the tougher role to play? In addition, haven't we all played both roles, in one lifetime or another?

What happens when the play is over? The members of the production all gather together for a cast party, do they not? The players congratulate each other for a job well-done. That actor who played the role of the evil villain? He's such a great actor—he really had me fooled: *I almost believed that he was not my brother.*

All Beings are on the Spiral of Light; all are on the Eternal Return back to the Creator. Some are taking a quicker, more direct route than others; but, all are headed back to the same Source. This is true of each and every Being—even if that Being doesn't believe that it is so, or intends otherwise. Give the dark warriors an opportunity to move up the Spiral with you. They can accept or reject the offer—that is their free-will choice. However, the offer must be made. Love your enemies.

Your creators, at Humanity's inception, gifted you with 12 strands of DNA operative—making you a 10th-dimensional being in the 3rd dimension. The evil snake in the Garden of Eden, the Annunaki, is part of the Divine Plan. If Human Beings had been allowed to keep all of their 12 strands of DNA operative, *they would have been denied free-will choice*—as they would have had, as Creator Gods, no challenges to face. This would have gone against the very nature of evolution in the 3rd dimension, as discussed above. *You are here to "do the work"; there are no shortcuts up the Spiral of Light.*

Humanity's creators were, then—in their own way—just as responsible as the Annunaki for the ensuing darkness on Earth. And they have truly learned this lesson in non-intervention: no one is allowed to deny the free-will of another, no matter how well-meaning their intentions. This is one more reason why you must dispel any lingering notions that you may have that benevolent ETs are going to come and save you. We have already shown that they couldn't save you, even if they wanted to. You are now being told that they *don't want to.*

It's up to you to "do the work", or not. It's your free-will choice.

Chapter Six

Karma, Forgiveness, and the Law of Attraction

In this chapter, I attempt to clarify some common confusions regarding the nature of Karma and the true purpose of Human life on Earth. In the process, I touch upon how forgiveness relates to the subject of Karma.

There exists a commonly-held belief that Karma represents the idea of punishment for failure to learn—in this, or another, lifetime—one's "life lessons". In truth, there are no "lessons" that you should, or must, learn. Instead, you are here to make free-will choices, and to have the experiences that follow, as a result of the Law of Attraction, from those choices. In creating/attracting those experiences, you contribute to the expansion of All That Is. To be sure, in the having of those experiences, you will learn (if nothing else, you will learn which experiences you prefer, and which ones you do not). However, the learning that takes place is a side-product of the having of the experiences, and *not* the reason for the experiences.

The suffering that, through your free-will choices, you may choose to experience does not represent punishment. As we have previously discussed, your Higher Self is the actual mechanism that creates/attracts your experiences, but it does so only in accordance with your consciously-held beliefs (or, equivalently, in accordance with what you have been predominantly thinking about/focusing your attention upon). Your Higher Self is not punishing you; it is returning to you, as your physical reality, the *precise vibrational essence* that you have freely-chosen to offer.

Thus, Karma represents being out-of-alignment with your Higher Self; that is, it is thinking about/focusing your attention upon that which you do *not* prefer to experience.

"Resolving your Karma", then, is simply choosing to think about/focus your attention upon that which you *do* prefer to experience.

Note that your Higher Self is always giving you guidance, in the form of your emotions, as to the appropriateness or inappropriateness of whatever you are currently thinking about/focusing your attention upon. That is, if what you are currently thinking about/focusing your attention upon would, were it to manifest, be something that you *would* enjoy, your Higher Self will communicate that fact to you by sending you *positive* emotion. Conversely, if what you are currently thinking about/focusing your attention upon would, were it to manifest, be something that you would *not* enjoy, your Higher Self will let you know this by sending you *negative* emotion. Simply by paying attention to how you feel, and by always reaching for the best-feeling thought you have access to in the moment, you do not "create new Karma" and, also, you "resolve Karma".

As we have seen previously, to stop creating/attracting experiences that you do not prefer, you do not need to do anything other than create/attract experiences that you do prefer.

The way in which forgiveness (of yourself and others) can help to resolve Karma is this: by forgiving, you are enabled to *stop* thinking about/focusing your attention upon that which you do *not* prefer to experience. Thus, are you enabled to *begin* thinking about/focusing your attention upon that which you *do* prefer to experience.

In order to bring yourself to the point where you are *willing* to forgive yourself or others, it may be helpful to remember that, through your free-will choices as to what to think about/focus your attention upon, you are the inviter of your life experiences. Knowing this, it becomes easier to realize that you are, neither, a victim nor a victimizer—and neither is anyone else. In truth, no one, including you, has done anything that they need to be forgiven for. This understanding makes it easy to shift your thoughts/ the focus of your attention from what you do not prefer to what you do.

So, let not your heart be troubled.

Chapter Seven

Rise of the Divine Feminine: Restoration of Balance

In this chapter, I discuss the imbalance on Earth between the male and female polarities. This imbalance must be rectified if Humanity is to move into the Golden Age as an ascended 4th Density civilization. As people begin to deliberately, consciously create the lives that they wish to experience, the balance will be naturally restored.

Separation of man from woman is but one aspect of the larger scheme of the World Management Team's playbook for managing Humanity and Earth's resources: divide and conquer; divide and rule. As long as men and women view each other as inferiors, property, rivals, or (even) enemies, there will be no peace on the planet, or in the home. Relationships between men and women, to be truly loving and supportive, must be formed between individuals who are, each, whole and complete within themselves.

Many men, today, have a block in their 2nd chakras, their feeling centers. Historically, this block has enabled men to do things that they likely would never have done if the blockage was not present. If you do not feel, you will not have empathy for others. For example, this block at the level of the navel chakra permits men to act without feeling: to make war; to torture; to rape; to plunder the Earth; and to support organizations that carry out such activities. To the Cabal/Illuminati, this has enabled them to recruit men into aiding them in the building and maintenance of their empires.

Many women, today, have a block in their 5th chakras, their communication centers. Historically, this block has enabled women to stand by and witness—without protesting—things that they likely never would have countenanced if the blockage was not present. Why do more women not express more disapproval of some of the activities of some of the men—activities such as war; torture; rape; and the plunder of the Earth? This blockage at the level of the throat chakra in women has served the Cabal/Illuminati in that it enables them to recruit men for their empire-building and –maintenance activities, without having women sabotage their efforts to do so (by providing to men an opposing viewpoint).

This dynamic of men having a blockage at the level of their feeling centers, and women having a blockage at the level of their communication centers, has created a situation on the planet where women are being treated as the inferiors of men, expected to say nothing while men run the organizations that dominate the planet. This has become a male-dominated planet, lacking harmony and balance between the male and female polarities. How can Humanity enter the Golden Age of an ascended 4th Density civilization with half of the Human population in subjection? It cannot.

As more and more men (and boys) and women (and girls) begin to consciously create their own (preferred) life experiences, the limiting beliefs that are being reflected back to them as lack of feeling (in men) and lack of empowerment to speak one's truth (in women) will begin to fade away. As their beliefs change—as what they are predominantly thinking about/focusing their attention upon changes--their realities will change to reflect the new beliefs. As men gain practice in paying attention to how they feel, and in always reaching for the best-feeling thought that they have access to in the moment, they will strengthen and expand their feeling centers (the 2nd chakra). Further, as men become allowers, they give permission to those around them, including women, to speak their truths. This will give women more practice in strengthening and expanding their communication centers (the 5th chakra).

A man who is consciously creating the life that he prefers is whole and complete within himself. *This wholeness is reflected in the fact that he is an allower.* Only such a man is capable of having a true, heart-centered union with another. He does not expect his partner to complete him, nor does he lead her to believe that she must depend upon another for her happiness. And the same is true for a woman: a woman who is consciously creating the life that she prefers is whole and complete within herself. She does not look to another to complete her. She is no longer tolerating that which she does not approve of, for fear of speaking her truth. Instead, she is an allower. Only such a woman is capable of having a true, heart-centered union with another.

As more and more people become deliberate, conscious creators of their own life experiences, they will come to pay more attention to the voice—the emotional guidance—of their Higher Selves. By paying attention to how they feel, and by always reaching for the best-feeling thought that they have access to in the moment, they are paying attention to the more intuitive—the *yin*, or female—aspect of themselves. This means, at the same time, that they are paying less heed to their Conscious Minds—the analytical, *yang*, or male aspect of themselves. As the Higher Self is directly connected to Source it is, literally, Divine ("of God"). Hence, as more and more people become deliberate, conscious creators of their own life experiences, more of the Higher Self—the Divine Feminine—is expressed onto the Earth plane. *This* will restore the balance, the harmony between man and woman on this planet.

Chapter Eight

Maldek and the Inner Earth

In this chapter, I will discuss the origin of the Inner Earth and its inhabitants. Some of these Beings will be interacting with surface Humanity (*Homo sapiens*) upon the New Earth.

The origin of non-*Homo sapiens* Humanoid lifeforms in the Inner Earth goes back to the days of Maldek (approximately, 30-45 million years ago). Insectoid and Reptilian lifeforms in the Inner Earth are even more ancient: from approximately 85-90 million years ago). So, to understand the Humanoid lifeforms of Agartha requires some background history pertaining to Maldek.

Maldek was the third planet in this Solar System (Saturn was first; Jupiter was second). Five large moons, and several smaller moons, orbited around Maldek (which was approximately one-half the size of Jupiter). The five large moons were, each, brought to this Solar System from other star systems. Today, you know those five large moons as the planets Mercury, Venus, Earth, Mars, and Ceres.

Upon Maldek and its five large moons were six root races of Humanoids (five races similar to those currently found on the surface of the Earth, plus a sixth, pale blue-skinned race). It was foreseen by the Confederation of Planets (the Saturnian Council) that it was probable that Maldek would destroy itself. So, the Council moved the large moons away from Maldek, in order to try to preserve as much of the life on those moons as possible. In the subsequent explosion of Maldek, the smaller moons were destroyed, right along with Maldek. Together, their remnants form what we, today, call the Asteroid Belt.

Prior to the destruction of Maldek and its smaller moons, some Humanoid Beings from Venus went to the Earth and established themselves underground, there. Bear in mind that, at that time, there already existed Insectoid and Reptilian lifeforms there. In fact, it was through the terraforming activities of these Insectoid Beings that the physical structure of Inner Earth was created. The tunneling activities of these Beings created honeycomb-like clusters within the interior of the Earth. The Humanoid Beings have, subsequently, utilized those large vaults in which to build their cities (which are, in fact, holographic).

So, there were Humanoid (and Primate) occupants, along with indigenous Insectoid, Reptilian, and other occupants, of Inner Earth long before *Homo sapiens* was created.

The Inner Earth Beings act as stewards of the Earth. All 2nd and 3rd Density lifeforms on the surface of the Earth are created within the Inner Earth, and delivered to the surface. The surface of the planet is to be left to 3rd Density lifeforms, that they may acquire an understanding of, and appreciation for, Nature (1st and 2nd Density life). Once those 3rd Density lifeforms reach 4th Density—and assuming that they have achieved a love of Nature—then, they may move into the Earth's interior with the Beings of Inner Earth.

Some of the Inner Earth Beings have, in the past, waged war upon one another. As a consequence, the Inner Earth is divided into territories that, in some ways, resemble countries on the surface of the Earth. Although some Inner Earth civilizations engage in trade and other friendly relations with other Agarthan groups, some of the Inner Earth Beings are not interested in interacting with others.

An agreement was reached, at the time of the Second Cycle of Atlantis, between the Inner Earth Beings and certain extraterrestrial groups (for example, the Yzhnuni from the 6th Density of Sirius B) to aid *Homo sapiens*, on the surface of Earth, with conscious crystalline technology.

Prior to the destruction of Maldek, some of the Annunaki left Maldek and established themselves underground upon Mars. From their base on Mars, these Beings came to Earth in the Third Cycle of Atlantis. These Beings contributed to the corruption of part of the Atlantean priesthood, which had control over the conscious crystalline technology. The crystalline technology was misused in a way that led to the destruction of much of the surface life on Earth (in some ways, similar to the way in which, today, HAARP technology is misused).

Needless to say, the Yzhnuni and the Inner Earth groups withdrew the conscious crystalline technology from *Homo sapiens.* Surface Humanity was not responsible enough at that time (and, to this day) to handle that kind of power without misusing and abusing it.

If, and when, you will ever be loving enough to handle that kind of power responsibly is up to you.

Chapter Nine

The Repopulation of Earth

In this chapter, I will explain how the Human population of Earth has been for some time, is now being, and will continue to be, transformed from within. The objective of this transformation of Humanity is to transform Human civilization into a more loving, Earth-friendly, and life-affirming society.

On July 16, 1945, the first atomic bomb was exploded at the Trinity Test Site in Alamogordo, New Mexico. Unbeknownst to most people at the time, the signal from the detonation was felt across the entire Universe. The World Management Team would now possess the ability, once the atomic arsenal was expanded, to destroy all life on Earth.

Additionally, and unknown to most Humans, atomic explosions actually penetrate to *other dimensions*, and damage or destroy lifeforms in those dimensions. The Cabal/Illuminati would now possess the means to harm or destroy off-planet entities, especially when atomic bombs are married to powerful rockets (technology that Humans were also evolving). Clearly, the "game of limitation" was threatening to involve others.

As if these implications of the advancement in the technology of war were not enough to cope with, the Cabal/Illuminati and their minions throughout the governments of the nuclear powers could wield the threat of nuclear annihilation as a sword of Damocles hanging constantly over the heads of the Human population of Earth. This would serve their purposes in a number of ways, including inducing an all-pervasive climate of fear on the planet. Additionally, the nuclear arms race could be used as a justification for funneling massive amounts of money from the public into the secret budgets of various "black" projects. Further, what better excuse could be found for justifying the need to launch out into space (in their quest to conquer the Moon and Mars), or to build enormous underground military installations, laboratories, and shelters? Or, for establishing a reign of secrecy, in which their activities could flourish? Or, in curtailing civil liberties?

Benevolent extraterrestrial and non-physical Beings understood, at the time, the ramifications of the Trinity explosion. Clearly, something had to be done, but what? After all, non-intervention is the order of this Universe.

So, Divine Dispensation was sought, and granted, for two main types of intervention into the affairs of Humans on Earth. First, although small-scale use of nuclear (or other) weapons would not be interfered with, any Human activity that threatened the existence of Mankind, as a collective, or the Earth, as a viable ecological system, would not be allowed. This is why ET spacecraft routinely appear near nuclear (and other) weapons sites: they are monitoring all matters pertaining to the designing, testing, building, transport, storage, deployment, and use of such weapons. They have actively intervened, in a number of instances, in the attempt to use such weapons—and they will continue to do so. Indeed, *every* single government on Earth has been explicitly told, by benevolent ETs, that they are not to use such weapons on a mass scale. Despite the fact that the World Management Team continues to spend public money on nuclear arsenals, and to threaten to use nuclear weapons (and other weapons of mass destruction), they *all* know that their threats are hollow. Such behavior is merely to impress and frighten—and make money off of—the public.

The second avenue of intervention authorized by the Creator was the repopulation of Earth. That is, loving Spirits from all over the Universe would be allowed to incarnate as Human Beings on Earth, in large numbers, in order to shift the vibration of Humanity in the direction of living peacefully with one another and with the Earth. Starting right after the beginning of the atomic era, each succeeding generation of Humans would be a little more advanced—in terms of genetics and lovingkindness—than the previous generation.

Four "waves" of such children have been born. The first, known as "Wayshowers", appeared in the 1950s and 1960s. The Wayshowers were more-inclined than most of their fellow Humans to seek Spiritual understanding through ancient paths, such as meditation and mediumship. In doing so, they were able to open the eyes of succeeding generations to the possibilities inherent in such practices.

The second wave of children, known as the "Indigo Children", were born in the 1960s and 1970s. As the name suggests, these children (many of whom are still alive, as adults) are more-capable of using their 6th chakra (the brow chakra) and, thus, are more-capable of accessing Divine knowledge, than previous generations. This ability was enabled in them due to their advanced genetics. This advancement in genetics was facilitated through planetary alignments, galactic alignments, extraterrestrial adjustments of DNA and energy bodies, and by similar adjustments carried out by non-physical Beings.

The Indigos have expanded Man's understanding of the Spiritual in all fields of endeavor. From the healing arts to the understanding that all Human Beings are inextricably linked to one another and to the Earth, the Indigos have affected, and continue to affect, the consciousness of Mankind.

During the 1980s, 1990s, and up to about the Millennium, were born the "Children of the Violet Ray", the third wave. These children have such advanced genetics that they perceive and communicate nonlinearly. However, because most Humans alive today can only perceive and communicate linearly, such children (and some are now adults) have been labeled by society as "dysfunctional". They have routinely been diagnosed, by the medical profession, as having ADD, ADHD, Autism Spectrum Disorder, or Schizophrenia when, in fact, *they are not dysfunctional, at all.* Many of these children and adults can perceive multiple realities simultaneously and are, in fact, communicating with one another quite successfully, even if most Human Beings are incapable of perceiving that this is so. Indeed, many of the Violet Ray are capable of accessing their own past life memories, or those of others. These are psychically-gifted individuals.

The fourth wave, the "Rainbow Children", born post-Millennium, are Hybrid children who are born on Earth. Arcturians, Pleiadians, Sirians, Orions, Lyrans, Zetas, etc., have contributed DNA to these children. These children and young adults are such that they will seek to do no harm to other Humans, or to the Earth. They will seek to work and live in harmony with others and, so, will be instrumental—with the assistance of the Indigo and Violet Ray generations—in transforming the political and economic order on Earth. They will be leaders in the building of the New Earth.

Eventually, the Rainbow Children, who are Hybrids who were born on Earth, will welcome to Earth the Zeta Reticuli-Human Hybrids (who were not born, naturally, on Earth).

In the coming years, the Indigo, Violet Ray, and Rainbow generations will advance Human society in all ways, transforming the civilization into a more peaceful, Earth-friendly, and life-affirming one. Technologically, these generations will advance Man's understanding and capabilities in areas such as healing; space travel; education; agriculture; energy generation; pollution-abatement; etc..

Chapter Ten

The New Earth

In this chapter, I outline an alternative to our current, worldwide economic and political order. This alternative has the added benefit of allowing Humanity to satisfy the three principal requirements for Open Contact. Finally, I discuss a route for integration of Human civilization into the Galactic community as an ascended 4th Density civilization.

The path that Humanity is currently on is unsustainable and, if pursued much further, can only lead to self-destruction. The structures that dominate the economic and political lives of Human Beings on planet Earth are unfixable and must be replaced. The dominant political systems of Earth are hopelessly corrupt. The dominant economic system—the money system—by its very nature, must pursue profit and, in that pursuit, will inevitably complete—unless stopped soon—the destruction of the planet. What is to be done?

What follows is merely an outline of one *possible* future for Humanity and Gaia. Which future manifests will be *your* free-will choice. Remember: to choose not to choose is, also, to choose (it is to choose the status quo; it is to choose self-destruction). You cannot escape choice.

Any viable political and economic system must meet three objectives. First, it must allow each individual Human Being to follow his/her own joy. Second, it must enable Human Beings, in political and economic terms, to take care of each other. Third, it must enable Human Beings to take care of the Earth.

The only known political and economic system that can accomplish these three objectives is

UBUNTU/Contributionism. What is UBUNTU/Contributionism?

In summary, it is an economic and political system in which money, barter, and trade play no role. Instead, there are Community projects in which each able-bodied member of the Community participates for a total of two hours per day. The products of these Community projects—be it water, food, shelter, electricity, health care, education—are available free-of-charge to all members of the Community. The remaining 22 hours of the day, the members of the Community are free to follow their own, individual passions.

It is understood that each person is the creator/attractor of his/her own reality and, thus, is sovereign in the affairs of his/her own life. All issues affecting the Community as a whole are decided in Community meetings in which all members of the Community directly participate. All decisions are arrived at by consensus. There exist Facilitators whose sole function it is to connect those who have goods and services to those who need them. As members of the Community, over time, come to trust their synchronicity, the Facilitators will no longer be necessary.

Note that UBUNTU/Contributionism allows the three requirements for Open Contact to be satisfied: to be more loving to each other; to the Earth; and to our Inner Earth brothers and sisters. UBUNTU/Contributionism allows Humanity to carry out, in political and economic terms, its stewardship responsibilities.

Once the three requirements for Open Contact are met, Humanity will be allowed to join, as a candidate member, a Galactic-level organization called the Association of Worlds (AoW). This organization will offer mentoring to Humans regarding how to function as a 4th Density Galactic civilization.

Various benevolent extraterrestrial civilizations will make Open Contact with Humanity. One of the first of these, if not the first, will be the Ya'yel civilization. The Ya'yel are one of the five Zeta Reticuli-Human Hybrid races and are among those ETs who are most-similar to Human Beings. Some of the Zeta-Human Hybrids will, eventually, come to live on Earth with Humans. In addition, Open Contact will involve the establishment of friendly relations with the civilizations of Agartha. With Open Contact will, also, come the recognition that two species of ETs have been living on Earth with Humans all along—namely, the dolphins and whales. As a consequence of this recognition, Humans will develop more friendly and extensive relationships with these Cetacean Beings.

Over the next one thousand years or so, much of Humanity will head for the stars. The Pleiades; Sirius; Orion; Arcturus; Lyra; and Alpha Centauri; are just *some* of the destinations that Humans will seek, becoming, in the process, the extraterrestrials of the future. As Humanity heads away from its birthplace, others will come to Earth to enjoy the beauty of this blue-green planet. Eventually, the Human physical body will be phased-out as the "standard issue" for those who choose to incarnate on Earth. Instead, entities incarnating on Earth will incarnate in one of the Zeta-Human Hybrid physical bodies.

As a stepping-stone to the stars, Humans will, first, come to live in spacecraft, or in orbiting platforms, above the surface of the Earth. This will leave the planet's surface free for Nature (1st and 2nd Density lifeforms) and for new 3rd Density life (for example, some of the Great Apes on Earth are, currently, 3rd Density, although this fact is not widely-known).

Additionally, over the next three hundred years or so, Humans may have the opportunity to participate in the "terraforming" of the surfaces of, first, Mars and, then, Venus. These projects would involve the transfer of some plant and animal specimens from Earth to those planets. This is fitting, as most of the plants and animals currently on Earth were, first, on Venus and, then, on Mars before being transferred to Earth.

In order for Humanity to graduate from candidate membership in the AoW to full membership in that organization, it will have to pass a "test". Humanity will have to demonstrate that it has learned how to be a Galactic civilization by acting as mentors for another, evolving race. That race, which has already been selected, lives on the third planet orbiting the Barnard star. Interestingly, many of the Human Beings currently on Earth who choose not to ascend to the 4th Density Earth will, after their lives come to a close on 3rd Density Earth, incarnate on the third planet orbiting the Barnard star. Thus, many of the Beings that 4th Density Humans will be mentoring will be their fellow brothers and sisters from 3rd Density Earth.

As stated, the above is just *one* possible timeline for Humanity and Earth. The future is yours to decide.